Concert and Contest COLLECTION

Solo B♭ Cornet-Trumpet
(Baritone Treble Clef)

T0071572

Compiled and Edited by H. VOXMAN

for

B♭ CORNET, TRUMPET OR BARITONE with piano accompaniment

CONTENTS

RUBANK®

HAL•LEONARD®
CORPORATION
7777 W. BLUEMOUND RD. P.O. BOX 13819 MILWAUKEE, WI 53213

Sarabanda and Gavotta

Bb Cornet or Trumpet
(Baritone 𝄞)

A. CORELLI
Edited by H. Voxman

Dedication
(Zueignung)

Bb Cornet or Trumpet
(Baritone 𝄞)

RICHARD STRAUSS, Op. 10, No. 1
Transcribed by H. Voxman

Premier Solo de Concours

Bb Cornet or Trumpet
(Baritone 𝄞)

RENÉ MANIET
Edited by H. Voxman

Calm As the Night

Bb Cornet or Trumpet
(Baritone 𝄞)

CARL BÖHM
Edited by H. Voxman

Andante and Allegro

B♭ Cornet or Trumpet
(Baritone 𝄞)

ROBERT CLÉRISSE
Edited by H. Voxman

Romance in Eb

Bb Cornet or Trumpet
(Baritone 𝄞)

LEROY OSTRANSKY

Air Gai

B♭ Cornet or Trumpet
(Baritone 𝄞)

G. P. BERLIOZ
Edited by H. Voxman

Orientale

Bb Cornet or Trumpet
(Baritone 𝄞)

J. Ed. BARAT
Edited by H. Voxman

Élégie

Bb Cornet or Trumpet
(Baritone 𝄞)

ALEXANDRE J. DUQUESNE
Edited by H. Voxman

Serenade

Bb Cornet or Trumpet
(Baritone 𝄞)

OSKAR BÖHME, Op. 22, No. 1
Edited by H. Voxman

My Regards

Bb Cornet or Trumpet
(Baritone 𝄞)

EDWARD LLEWELLYN
Edited by H. Voxman

L'Allegro
(The Merry Man)

Bb Cornet or Trumpet
(Baritone 𝄞)

PAUL KOEPKE

Petite Pièce Concertante

Bb Cornet or Trumpet
(Baritone 𝄞)

GUILLAUME BALAY
Edited by H. Voxman

Morceau de Concours

B♭ Cornet or Trumpet
(Baritone 𝄞)

G. ALARY, Op. 57
Edited by H. Voxman

Concertino

Bb Cornet or Trumpet
(Baritone 𝄞)

LEROY OSTRANSKY

Andante
from Concerto in E♭

B♭ Cornet or Trumpet
(Baritone 𝄞)

F. J. HAYDN
Edited by H. Voxman